HEART AND SOUL

LEVEL 1

INTEGRATION SYSTEM

DJ Green

TABLE OF CONTENTS

QUALITY REIGN SUPREME

FOREWORD

Throughout time, there have been many attempts for Man to understand and tangibly grasp either mentally or physically the ethereal or supernatural worlds. It has been at the forefront of our collective minds since the time we first began to wonder. I have always been a person of wonder. I became a person interested in seeing the potential in myself and the things around me. This led me to read and investigate many systems, read ancient books, hope to visit gurus, and the like, but I could not help but feel that there seemed to be something missing.

The teachers seemed to have knowledge, but there was definitely a question of authenticity in the back of my mind. Do we walk what we talk? Do we live what we teach? Is this person on a power trip? The answers were too hard to tell, but as luck would have it, the creator or some existential force saw fit to take my hand and lead me to a group of seekers and fearless explorers of themselves and the subtle fields permeating our reality. All of us were beginners on this path together, and together we walked into this unknown abyss and reached out into the void and found a gracious hand reaching back for us, a peaceful hand to coach us, and a joyful hand to enliven us!

Throughout our experimentations and revelations, Donald Green, affectionately known as DJ, was at the forefront. As some of us lost focus in our daily lives, he kept the torch lit so we could always find our way back, and through the carrying of that torch, he had illuminated himself and those around him to the level of ascended ancestor even before we transitioned. Truly amazing!

I am truly grateful and honored to have been asked to provide these foregoing words. The techniques and insights offered in this book have the ability—if you have the diligence—to help you integrate the many levels of your being and bodies into one another and, more importantly, grants access at will to these higher bodies. Be warned, this system is NOT for your self-aggrandizement! It is NOT to inflate your ego! This system is for those who are truly and authentically looking to know themselves and possibly break the cycles that have been haunting you and your family line for generations.

This information has no religious affiliation or cultural bias. This system is of true self-love, self-reflection, and release. Misuse could equal misfortune...stranger things have happened. Lastly, I want to congratulate you on coming in contact with this book. There are bits and pieces of this information scattered between different systems on different continents, but very few include practical action steps to achieve the outcome described in the holy books. This is your manual/workbook to your heart's door and the many vast applications lying therein. This information is not theoretical, nor is this a book of lofty ideas that no man shall ever attain. Every person can succeed in these exercises. Take your time and change your life! Greater Good Fortune!

- Adara Moselle

QUALITY REIGN SUPREME

ADVICE

The wisdom of the heart is the ultimate intuition. We perish in so many ways due to not living by the intelligence of the heart, which would keep us on track with our divine purpose. The core of the soul speaks out to the pathway of integration (energy bodies, quantum fields, etc.) by way of the heart. Through integration, this path will free your heart, mind, and soul by placing them into proper alignment in a gentle way. Allowing your natural gifts to become more active in your life. And, in turn, you begin to realize the many aspects of your divinity.

Being courteous of the details is advised. Please don't harm yourself by trying to force things to happen when you would like when it comes to these steps. You must grasp the endeavored experience in your spirit to let you know when it's time to move on to the next step. As your intuition increases, you will begin to see yourself and the world clearly. Remember, not everyone will see what you see. Do not force it upon people; it may hurt them in ways that you cannot understand for a while. Cherish your "new-found gifts" coming back to you. The experiences only get better as you move forward with the exercises. For some, "tornados" will come tearing apart the falsities of your life—things that are not naturally for you—i.e., false relationships, type of work, diet, beliefs, etc. and will present situations for you to make the correction.

Genetic codes are rewritten by doing this marvelous work. Shapes will appear, guiding and shifting you. It's up to you to let go of things that stifle you. It takes a lot of courage to walk down this path, but your soul needs it. We as people need it to help elevate each other and the Earth with higher frequency. Discharge your bullshit into the hands of the alchemist—YOU— and take it where it's needed. The core fundamental teaching will serve you in everyday life with your family, friends, co-workers, associates, and environment. It will emanate out of you. This is not an easy road for some. We cherish those who do take this to heart and make a change that will benefit the world. Come one, come all if you are ready, start walking towards yourself. Peace, be humble.

Note: continuum from source. The wise caters to the emotions, energetic change and effects on the body while performing these practices.

WHY WORK ON THE HEART?

The importance of getting rid of clutter in the heart increases your clairaudience, clairsentience, claircognizance, and clairvoyance, among many other things. Freeing the heart of clutter enables you to see who you truly are in this macro/microcosm of infinity and to know your rightful place of what you can do, where you should be, and how to get there. You can have the infinite ability to reach connections with so much more pleasure and uniqueness and know how to weather the storms with sound advice, harmony, and grace. You will know how to connect to really touch someone at their depths of what there being needs. Eventually, you will easily control your emotions while having them work for you to experience true peace on another level many have not experienced. But this will help cultivate your soul while bringing new experiences into your life.

Getting rid of the clutter also helps the heart function properly to express itself. The heart will tell you how to respond in certain situations that are best for you. However, we have to let go of the ridged stubbornness, self-esteem issues, hurt, and pain in order for the heart to flourish and your being to integrate. By following your heart more than following your ego, the integration of your selves will begin to take place. One of the many signs that the integration has started is when the heart feels lighter and expansive, which we will get into later. You will bring more sustenance to your friendships through inner and outer-standing of yourself. You will be able to recognize when the counterfeit personality of your ego is at play more clearly. Courage becomes easier the more clutter you get rid of and the wiser you get. I will expound more with the experiences you might have the more work you put into self.

RESPOND TO THE HEART

R esponding to the heart allows you to know the real you, as well as the things you really need and don't need. You will be able to distinguish between your feelings and emotions, and whether or not and how to respond to a situation based on the feelings of your heart or emotions related to your type of ego. The more you respond to your heart after clearing it, the more active your soul becomes. For most of us, it will take some time because we are usually fully operating in our ego. The heart knows what you should and should not eat, when to sleep, and who to be with relationship-wise. It knows how to address situations and how to change the energy in any environment if needed. The heart brings a higher quality to your life if you choose to listen and act upon it for your overall wellbeing.

Keep in mind, the heart has 40,000 neurons that the divine intelligence communicates through. Those whose egos have a very strong hold over them will struggle with this the most and find reasons not to pursue this inner path. Please don't abandon your mind. You will begin to recognize when to switch from the heart, brain, and gut, and, ultimately, bring the heart, brain, and gut into proper alignment. The heart will show you this through these teachings. Eventually, they will merge, and you will have a higher quality of life, which will indirectly affect everyone around you as your frequency raises. Spiritual growth is not always pretty—much of it would be considered ugly to some but necessary for you, your family, tribe, and planet. Responding to your heart is the inner path to divine wisdom, which will begin to emerge out of the shadows. Through the heart is where you find your quintessential essence of the immortal. You will learn more about this and what comes with it. Your heart can act as a beacon, letting you know what's going on in certain environments and how to respond.

CORRESPONDENCE

Correspondence between the heart's interaction with the soul by way of its continuum provides great heart connections, greater intercourse, and greater understanding. Inattention might take place, but with greater understanding, deeper intimate connection will occur. You will begin to move heavens and earth easily learning correspondence. Forces will prevail and initiate the understanding of the last sentence. Catering to the heart and soul of women/men is where life's journey of inner workings truly begins, and this affects the world beyond what the eyes can see.

Bless his/her soul for the outcome they reach. Teach others the meaning of spontaneous joy from within. Shine as the sun's rays uncovering the darkness that hides things in its shadows which fears exposure. Even though it is harmless, it is dangerous to your wellbeing due to the lack of emotional stability.

Correspondence of your quintessential essence of the immortal will teach you the true meaning of your soul's purposes, amongst many other things related to the soul and beyond. Once your innate being learns to unwind, you can really be taught kindness, geometrical, mathematical, and equation that shakes and rocks this earth. It all starts with the joy you create in your heart—not false joy but pure, eternal joy! You will not succumb to anything of a lesser vibration. You will be too strong, and it will antagonize these lower frequency entities.

QUALITY REIGN SUPREME

GENERATING

Generating from the heart becomes easier the more time you spend in your heart. Just from having a thought drop down into the heart and watch it spread outwardly after being internalized. Almost anything can be generated from the heart, whether it's healing or manifesting. The heart is the power center. The heart is where infinite intelligence dwells and the answer to all your questions—the access point to all that seems very endless. There is power in generating from the heart, which is continuous and massive. It requires a great deal of pleasant attention and awareness. You have to get so comfortable that it becomes your second home from the home in your head.

Do not be controlled by your ego, as there is no freedom when it's necessary to explore places beyond the comforts of the ego. You will have to use courage, passion, and enlightenment, amongst many other things that the ego cannot attest to by itself.

Eventually, the ego will have to relinquish its power as long as you continue to step outside of your comfort zone and learn about your type of ego. You also learn there is a great deal of responsibility that comes with your growth. Generating from the heart is safer than elsewhere, and there are no negative side effects. The heart wants what the soul wants. Nowadays, the heart is in the forefront of the soul, but the brain is in front of the heart, and the ego is in the number-one spot.

AMALGAMATION

When the heart merges with the brain and gut, the subtle forces of the universe begin to bend at your will. The "I am" is in the heart. Ultimate power affects everything more than you could know in this lifetime, but with conscious effort, you will begin to know. Parallels, geometry, math is the language of the universe, which starts to reveal itself as you move more into the heart intelligence. When the clutter is cleared, you really begin to know oneself and others deeper than they know in some aspects of their lives. When generating from the heart, keep in mind, the ego will do whatever it can to distract you, so don't give up; it's another way for the ego to lose its footing along with whatever is attached to it.

FOUR SECTION

Transmutation - happens when the functions begin to change for the better or worse in all things of nature at your command. Spreading into the depths of atoms and molecules through energy signatures affecting many things all the way to matter.

Ridicule - causes embarrassment, hurt, pain, and sadness, whether you are on the receiving end or giving end.

Sustenance - has vitality, vigor, self-esteem, quality, and power.

Turmoil - brings about confusion, pain, anger, and grief.

MORE ADVICE

Exercise, healthy eating habits, and qigong on a regular basis are highly recommended while doing this internal work. It requires a lot of energy usage to grow as the divine being you are. Repetition and trance will transform signal passageways to break up old subconscious and conscious behavior, memories, and attachments while rewriting your genetic codes to assist in your integration of selves. You will start to feel yourself unravel emotionally as you purge and feel your other energy bodies, which may feel foreign. Keep in mind, the stronger your heart field becomes, you will begin to have an effect on the people close to you as well as your environment. Others will either become happy or angry, depending on what they choose when the energy arises in them. Sometimes your bioelectromagnetic field (aura) will agitate the attachments in their energy field, which will affect their behavior.

Remember, as you get stronger with this work, it is essential to be mindful of your thoughts, feelings, and actions due to your quality of frequency being of a higher vibration. Stay in your heart; follow your heart as much as possible when you are not performing these steps. This helps cultivate a relationship with your heart and soul, which will teach you the importance of quality emotional control and how the emotions affect you and others. Compassion will be a great lesson learned that will benefit you highly with these practices. The veil will slowly begin to lift. Know that you are powerful. Stay true to your heart/soul if you begin to feel unsure.

Your ego will try to stay in control at all costs, fighting to the very end, but it is no match for the heart and soul. Situations will come forward to test you in many different ways, but your heart will give you the answers you need to handle those situations. Going into the core steps with an open mind, not trying to control the outcome but going with the flow of your essence, will help tremendously. For some, this will not be an easy path emotionally, but it's worth it for everyone with whom you come in contact, especially the world.

This system will lead you to yourself as you begin to look for answers within rather than outside forces. Your ancestors and future family will also benefit from your use of this system.

THANK YOU SO MUCH!!!

PLEASE CONSULT A DOCTOR/PHYSICIAN BEFORE USING THESE PRACTICES.

QUALITY REIGN SUPREME

SUN/FORCES OF NATURE

We are all connected at the core due to mathematics being the language of the universe. Using your discernment, tapping into the four forces of nature will take you into the depths of the universe and teach you more about life. The forces of nature—gravitational, weak nuclear forces, the electromagnetic force, and strong forces—create structures. The relationship between the four forces of nature is based on the way particles deal with the force, the corresponding strength of the force, the distant effectiveness of force, and the character of the particles that referee the force. Each of these forces has a communication system that delivers the ramification and information to each other, Earth, and the bioelectromagnetic field of people and their DNA.

The blood carries so much information, it may take a lifetime to learn. The plasma that's in your blood contains some of the information along with transporting nutrients, proteins, minerals, and hormones, which plays a major part in your cells. Plasma also helps get rid of the chemical garbage from the cells by dissolving the substance the cells don't need and carries them away. With that being said, using the torus field, you have the power to change your DNA's algorithm, accessing and transporting information from your heart throughout the neurons. The energy fields around the neurons and heart send messages energetically wherever directed; for example, to the core of the universe or a loved one.

The best time to perform these exercises is during the day due to the sunlight's effects on boosting serotonin levels while simultaneously sending information. Serotonin is a chemical messenger, called a neurotransmitter, that acts on blood vessels and pain control pathways in the brain. It is also responsible for controlling mood, attention, sleep, and pain. Serotonin comes from a line of molecules that give off energy derived from the sun. A very high percentage of serotonin is made in the gut, brain, and blood platelets. Communication happens by way of the vagus nerve to the heart and brain.

This world has many realities and forces. As you clear the blockages that limit your use of neural transmitters, you begin to align with yourself, making it easier to learn how to access these different realities with the help of adinkra symbols (mathematical codes) discussed in string theory. That allows you access into other realities energetically. Raise your vibration to interact with these different adinkras by way of the energetic fields within and around yourself, i.e., forces of nature. Having high levels of joy, peace, and grace causes the neurons to wire together and access the adinkras in the field where the information lives to acquire that information, going beyond the different dimensions that most cannot comprehend.

MOVING BODY

Relax as you perform these exercises to allow your body to physically express itself. Your body may move subtly, strongly, or even go into various mudras such as Gyan, Anjali, Garuda, etc. Consecration will begin to happen. Pay attention with your awareness.

SOUNDS

The vibration of sound affects us in so many ways—some are subtle, and some are harsh. There are sounds we can make that help with our organs and nature. We are working with a few sounds for level 1 of the integration system that will help you tremendously while staying present in the heart, pushing outward from the heart loud, clear, and powerful with these sounds. You will also make these sounds silently from the heart. Start with five minutes on each sound out loud, then silently for five minutes each.

Haawww = heart, fire, light, joyous, content, and freedom.

Shu = dry air, wind, light, plasmasphere.

HHHAAAWWWWW! Out loud, repeatedly, for five minutes. Then repeat silently for five minutes.

SSSHHHUUUUUUU! Out loud, repeatedly, for five minutes. Then repeat silently for five minutes.

HA!...HA!...HA!...HA! Out loud, repeatedly, for five minutes. Then repeat silently for five minutes.

*Repeat this exercise at least three days a week for the next nine weeks.

COLORS

Everything in the Universe vibrates at different rates, including you, plants, animals, fruits, sound, colors, etc. Colors vibrate at different frequencies. Everything that vibrates has these adinkra signals in its energy field and can be accessed to shift the environment. When colors are introduced on a cellular level, they can be used to break up blockages (traumatic memories) and elevate feelings into a higher state of awareness. Here are a few basic colors to start with. As you advance, other colors are also necessary to use.

Blue = cell healing

Orange = clearing contamination

Green = growth

QUALITY REIGN SUPREME

Exercise 2

Relax every muscle in your body. Quiet your mind. Place your awareness on all three dantians. Dedicate at least twenty minutes a day putting your awareness on all three dantians. This exercise takes time, so be persistent. After a while, you will begin to tap into your soul. Your body may shake or tremble for a little bit. Once this happens, you will begin to feel things you never felt before. With awareness and feeling in all three dantians, ask your soul to purge itself of entities, past life trauma and connections that no longer serve you. The purging can manifest as emotional, energetic pain and bring up old situations for you to resolve while learning to deal with your emotions. For some, the emotional pain that comes up might be excruciating, but you are stronger than you realize. Nothing is more precious than your soul; never give it up. Do this exercise for at least nine weeks before moving on to the next one.

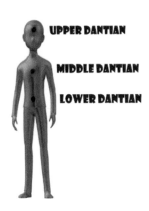

Upper Dantian – Center of the brain.

Middle Dantian – Through the center of the sternum close to the spine.

Lower Dantian – Through the navel close to the spine.

When going through the sections of the heart, pay attention to what comes up, such as past experiences. Determine what section it relates to, then acknowledge it, and explore the impact it has had on your life. When you are not performing these steps, hold the feeling in your heart as best as you can throughout the day and night, no matter what situation arises. This will help you obtain better emotional control when random emotions start to come up.

Integration System

1.   Transmutation (noun)—The action of changing or the state of being changed into another form.

    a.   (Physics)—The changing of one element into another by radioactive decay, nuclear bombardment, or similar processes.

    b.   (Biology)—The conversion or transformation of one species into another.

2.   Ridicule (noun)—The subjection of someone or something to contemptuous and dismissive language or behavior.

    a.   (verb)—Subject (someone or something) to contemptuous and dismissive language or behavior.

3.   Sustenance (noun)—The maintaining of someone or something in life or existence.

4.   Turmoil (noun)—A state of great disturbance, confusion, or uncertainty.

5.   Joy (noun)—A feeling of great pleasure and happiness.

6.   Peace (noun)—Freedom from disturbance; quiet and tranquility.

7.   Grace (noun)—Simple elegance or refinement of movement.

COHERENCE

Gently place your tongue on the roof of your mouth near the back of your teeth as you sit or lie still. Concentrate your awareness on your whole body, breath, and heartbeat. Inhale through your nose and exhale out your mouth while keeping your chest still but letting your stomach move out and in. Allow the relaxation to overcome your being, letting your body move however it pleases.

Shift your awareness to your heartbeat and rhythmically breathe to the count of nine heartbeats. This may be too long for some in the beginning, so do what feels comfortable for you starting out. For those who are more advanced, inhale for nine heartbeats, then, energetically in your heart, say, "Haww." Exhale for nine heartbeats and say, "Haww," energetically. Repeat till you feel one or two torus energy fields flowing through your heart in every direction simultaneously. By this time, you will be in semi or full trance. Once this happens, it is a great time to begin the core step to this practice.

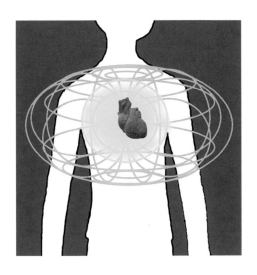

Now take a look at the images below, the back view of your heart. Shift your focus to the transmutation area of your heart by filling it up with either the feeling of joy, grace, or peace (use only one at a time, starting with joy). Remember, FEEL, FEEL, FEEL, and Feel! Let the inhalation from your nose travel down into the transmutation area and fill it up with joy, grace, or peace. Exhale. Continue until the transmutation area feels overwhelmed with the feeling of joy, grace, or peace. Once the overwhelming feeling occurs, inhale down into transmutation and, as you exhale, send the feeling of joy down into the ridicule area until it is filled up with each inhale and exhale. Then, inhale back into transmutation, holding the feeling of joy again. Once the overwhelming feeling is there, send the exhale up to the sustenance area until it is filled with joy. Once that's complete, return to transmutation filling it up with joy, grace, or peace till feeling overwhelmed. Once complete, on the exhale, send the feeling of joy, grace, or peace to the turmoil area until it feels overwhelmed with joy. Inhale back to the transmutation area, refilling it with joy.

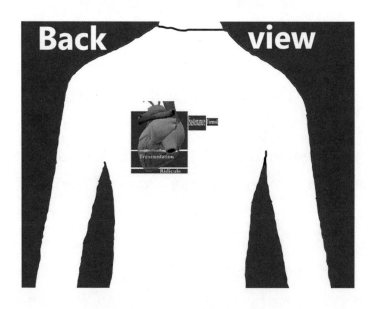

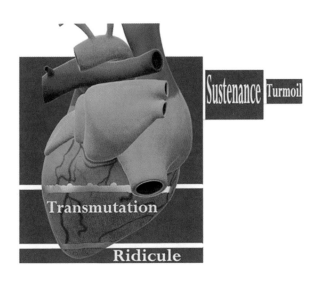

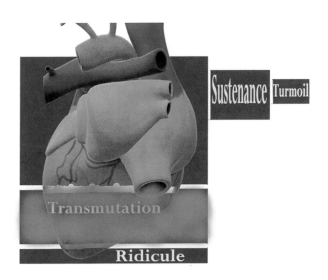

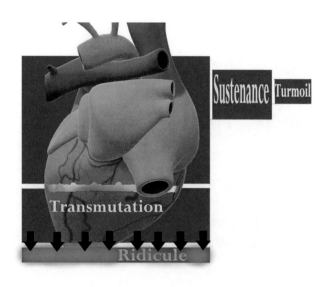

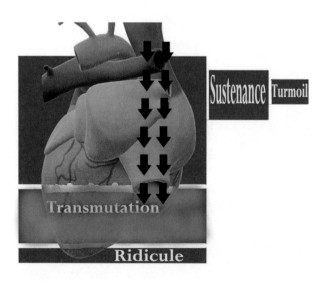

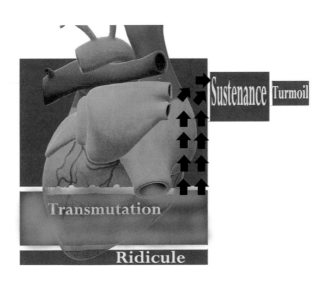

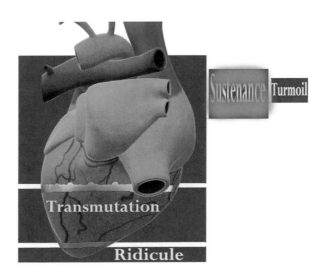

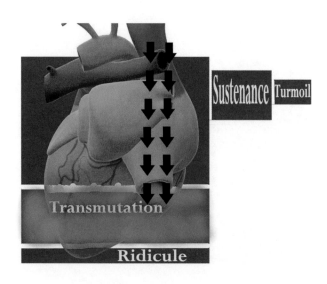

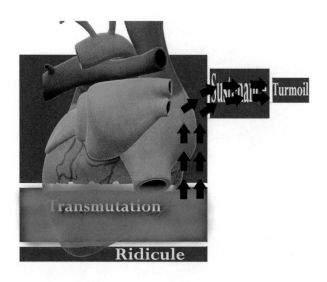

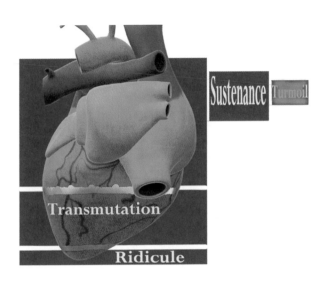

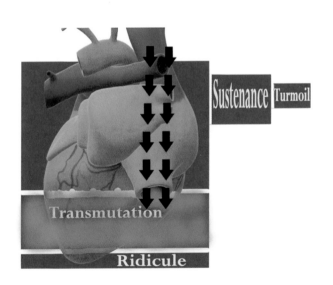

If you perform these core steps enough, you will eventually go into trance, and a hologram-like octahedron will appear in the front of your chest, more specifically, the sternum. Once the octahedron appears, gently turn the bottom half of the octahedron clockwise until you feel it cannot turn anymore or your intuition tells you to stop. Next, turn the top half of the octahedron counterclockwise until you cannot turn it anymore or intuition tells you otherwise. When this takes place, you might shake strongly. If this happens, do not worry; it will pass. Stay present in that moment until the octagon appears. The octagon represents the eight aspects of your soul with a circle in the middle. It will be in proper alignment due to you turning the octahedron correctly.

Note: When performing this procedure, you might feel aches and pains or tightness of the chest, which is normal. This is the blockage being broken up and leaving. The more you perform this, the more your body will begin to move and express itself. Allow this to happen. Different posture and prostrations will manifest (shaking, vibrating, mudras, etc.) Your body is shaking off the old and realigning itself energetically.

Note: The core step can be performed throughout the day minus going into trance.

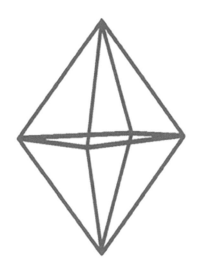

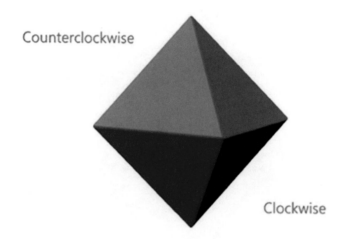

Counterclockwise

Clockwise

QUALITY REIGN SUPREME

When you fill the targeted area of your heart with a certain feeling while breathing slow and deep into the section continually, you begin to repair that section by removing the depths of blockage in that area. You will eventually create a suitable environment for your soul expansion and integration, among many other things, such as a new-found awareness with depths most neither have entered nor have the ability to comprehend. You are changing your epigenetics to give you a fresh start from ancestral habits that may hinder you in this lifetime. This is not an overnight process; this comes with personal tests on a much deeper level than you may realize. You will eventually bring your immortal essence to the forefront and embrace it along with your energy bodies and create easier with the forces of nature, but first, the heart must be cleared of its blockages to become energetically lighter and expansive, allowing light to fill the whole heart.

When performing these steps, you may feel very little, or nothing at all. KEEP GOING! In the beginning, you might not feel any energy flow, and that's okay. It will show in your day to day life. Some examples include random strangers speaking to you more, someone offering to pay for your gas at the pump, calls out of the blue from old friends/associates bringing closure to old situations, people complimenting you more than the usual, or animals responding to you differently. These are just a few examples, so please don't give up when things get tough.

CORE STEPS

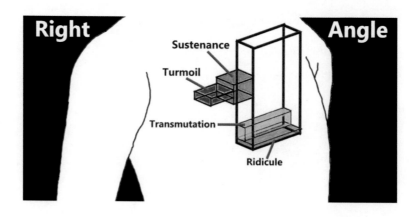

Right Angle

Sustenance
Turmoil
Transmutation
Ridicule

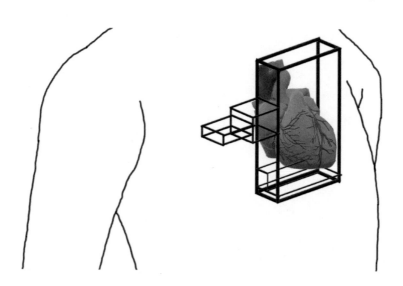

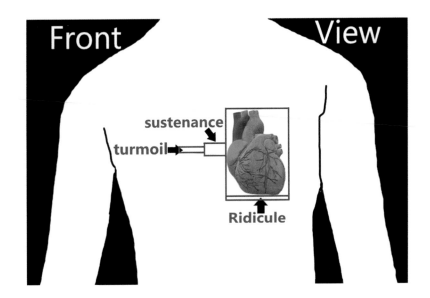

Front **View**

sustenance

turmoil

Ridicule

ALLOW YOURSELF TO GO INTO TRANCE

1. The transmutation area fills with joy on the inhale until you feel overwhelming joy in that area.

2. From the transmutation area, send joy to the ridicule area until there is no more ridicule.

3. From the transmutation area, send joy to the sustenance area until you feel stronger.

4. From the transmutation area, send joy to the turmoil area until it clears. (Most people have a hard time with this area.)

5. Refill the transmutation area with joy.

6. Once you feel the torus field appear in your heart as a tunnel or two tunnels with energy

flowing in unity in opposite directions simultaneously, this is the indwelling intelligence. It has a strong, peaceful essence to it. Congratulations!!! Begin to learn and explore this space. Remember what to do when the octahedron appears.

*Repeat steps 1-6 with joy a minimum of three times a week for nine weeks, then move on to the next steps.

7. The transmutation area fills with peace on the inhale until you feel overwhelming joy in that area.
8. From the transmutation area, send peace to the ridicule area until there is no more ridicule.
9. From the transmutation area, send peace to the sustenance area until you feel stronger.
10. From the transmutation area, send peace to the turmoil area until it clears. (Most people have a hard time with this area.)
11. Refill the transmutation area with peace.
12. Once you feel the torus field appear in your heart as a tunnel or two tunnels with energy flowing in unity in opposite directions

simultaneously, this is the indwelling intelligence. It has strong, peaceful essence to it. Congratulations!!! Begin to learn and explore this space. Remember what to do when the octahedron appears.

*Repeat steps 7-12 with peace for a minimum of three times a week for nine weeks, then move on to the next steps.

13. The transmutation area fills with grace on the inhale until you feel overwhelming joy in that area.

14. From the transmutation area, send grace to the ridicule area until there is no more ridicule.

15. From the transmutation area, send grace to the sustenance area until you feel stronger.

16. From the transmutation area, send grace to the turmoil area until it clears. (Most people have a hard time with this area.)

17. Refill the transmutation area with grace.

18. Once you feel the torus field appear in your heart as a tunnel or two tunnels with energy flowing in unity in opposite directions

simultaneously, this is the indwelling intelligence. It has strong, peaceful essence to it. Congratulations!!! Begin to learn and explore this space. Remember what to do when the octahedron appears.

*Repeat steps 13–18 with peace for a minimum of three times a week for nine weeks.

Note: Take your time building up joy, grace, or peace, whichever one you are working with, until it feels overwhelming in the transmutation, ridicule, sustenance, and turmoil areas.

Note: Do not try to force the torus field to appear; let it come on its own.

Try incorporating these colors into the core steps as well:

Inhale blue into the transmutation area, then push blue down to ridicule. Inhale orange to transmutation area, then send orange into the sustenance area. Inhale green into the transmutation area, then send it to turmoil area.

*Green = growth, orange= healing contamination, blue= cell healing.

1. Inhale blue into the transmutation area, then send blue to ridicule.
2. Inhale orange into the transmutation area, then send orange into the sustenance area.
3. Inhale green into the transmutation area, then exhale to turmoil area.

Repeat steps 1-6 infusing joy, grace, and peace for a minimum of three times a week for nine weeks.

QUALITY REIGN SUPREME

CORRAL YOUR SOUL

The Integration System helps the soul become more active by way of the heart. Most souls feel trapped, asleep, and disconnected. This is why it is of great importance to corral your soul for overall wellness. Having the soul in its rightful alignment will help you learn from the many aspects of your soul and brings more of your natural gifts to the forefront when needed. These divine teachings are intrusive of self on every level, but it's imperative to push forward. Eventually, the more you work on the heart and soul, the more the soul will illuminate.

After performing the core steps enough to clear out the sections of your heart, allow the hologram octahedron to appear. Do not force the appearance of the octahedron. Once the octahedron appears in front of our chest in direct alignment with your sternum, looking down at the octahedron hovering in front of your chest, slowly turn the bottom half clockwise until your intuition tells you to stop! Turn the top part counterclockwise until it meets at the same position that brings proper alignment to have access to your soul. Be patient and wait for an octagon to appear, which may take a while.

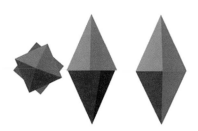

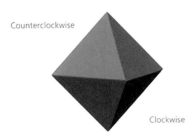

Counterclockwise

Clockwise

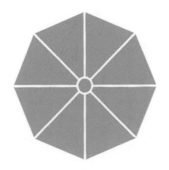

In the middle of the octahedron is an octagon-shaped flower, which represents eight aspects of the soul. The eight aspects are as follows: Sacred/Root, Correspondence/Shadow, Matter/Form, Time/Allowance, Body of the soul/Ba, Crescent/Over, Y/Y, and Enlightenment/Courage; in the middle is Immortal Essence/True spirit world. When the octagon-like flower appears, showing the eight aspects of your soul, continue holding the previous vibration of joy, grace, or peace in order to enter the aspects of the soul. Joy gives you access to sacred-root, body of the soul/ba, crescent/over, Y-Y, enlightenment/courage, and immortal essence/true spirit world. Grace gives access to correspondence/shadow and time/allowance. Peace gives access to matter/form and Y/Y.

In order, start at sacred/root, correspondence/shadow, matter/form, time/allowance, body of soul/ba, crescent/over, y/y and enlightenment/courage. I advise you to audio record or write down everything you see, hear, and learn once you come out of trance in each aspect. I HIGHLY recommend going into each section of your soul from the standpoint of observing, listening, and learning what's being revealed to you the first three times going around the soul before asking questions about what you should do in your day to day life. There is another way to talk to the entire soul for important information pertaining to your life. There will be great knowledge given to your benefit.

Also, when you have gone around your soul once, you will be able to access deeper layers into the soul and your immortal essence, which will give you access to the true spirit world. Awareness will increase once you go through the immortal essence. Knowledge of all will be clearer and safer through the higher faculties of your immortal essence. Your immortal essence is the fluid of the diamond light body. Once you've gone around all eight aspects of your soul while in trance, you can place yourself into the octahedron and go into the true spirit world through your immortal essence. Remember to knock gently when you get to a destination. Go around your soul at least three times. Remember to record what you learn.

Note: You can spend a lifetime exploring just one aspect of your soul. It's up to you if that is what you choose. I suggest going around your soul at least three times.

Note: I am not responsible for you once you get into your immortal essence and awaken the soul fully. Please take this seriously. Pay attention. You are being charged to do something because your sanity is at stake. It's advised not to go against your soul once it becomes more awakened.

IMMORTAL ESSENCE

IMMOARTAL ESSENCE
TRUE SPIRIT WORLD

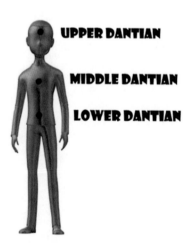

UPPER DANTIAN

MIDDLE DANTIAN

LOWER DANTIAN

Note: The other way to conversate with the soul for more information pertaining to daily life is to simultaneously tap into all three dantians through inhalation while asking pertinent questions.

After performing the core step as advised for the suggested weeks, you should be ready for the next exercise. Relax while you are standing with your legs shoulder-width apart. Inhaling slowly through the nose, deeply send your energy to the center of your Middle Dantian about three times while calling your immortal essence to the forefront internally in the Middle Dantian. Let your hands come together in prayer form at the Middle Dantian. Let the energy move your upper torso counterclockwise for about 50 plus circles. Inhale slowly through your nose, sending the energy to the center of your Top Dantian about three times, and allow your head to move around clockwise/counterclockwise while calling your immortal essence to the forefront internally in the Top Dantian. Inhale slowly through your nose, sending the energy down into the center of your Lower Dantian about three times while calling your immortal essence to the forefront internally in the Lower Dantian. Allow your lower body to move clockwise.

You will begin to feel an old inner presence come to the forefront. This is your "ancient self." Your quintessential essence of the immortal has arrived. Once that has happened, you can purge all carbon copies of "you" by simply saying, "I purge all carbon copies of myself." The real you can flow with the natural essence of the universe once you throw away those carbon copies of self and get to your real essence and work from your real power center. With action and visualization, go into the Middle Dantian to access your immortal essence to begin. You can also ask the name of your soul and its purpose, among other things. Heal or manifest by connecting energetically and holding the image with the feeling of the outcome you want for a period of time on a continuous basis—intuition will let you know. Don't accept anything less than your desired outcome. First, purge all copies of yourself so you can work from your real essence, which is your real power.

LET THE SUN POUR IN

The more you practice these steps, the more you will find yourself being outside in nature, in particular, in the sun, which has a major influence on oneself. The sun will help when performing the core steps along with the "meditation."

For this next exercise, close your eyes and keep them closed. Stand with your chest facing the sun. Inhale the rays of the sun through your Middle Dantian. Let the energy travel up your spine to your head as it moves clockwise in a circular motion around the top of your skull. Repeat 3x, then relax and go about your day. Do this at your own inclination. (Insert image)

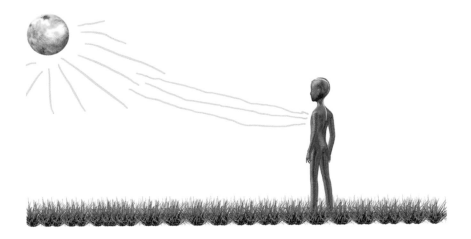

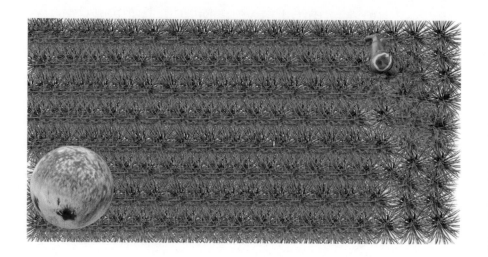

QUALITY REIGN SUPREME

ENERGY FIELD BEHIND THE STERNUM

Relax and feel the energy field behind the sternum. Spend time searching and learning about this area. Once you go through the core steps, inhale into the energy-strip-like quantum field, then exhale an octahedron out of it, covering your whole body. Begin your meditation inside the octahedron.

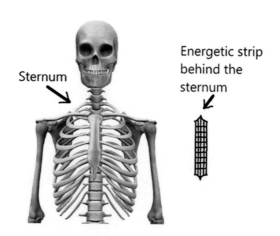

Sternum

Energetic strip behind the sternum

BRAIN, HEART, GUT

Once enough clearing of the heart is accomplished, the divine intelligence of the heart expresses itself into existence easier through the cell membranes, membranous sac, etc. The energy from the heart is spiraling up to the pineal gland, then expanding outward throughout the course of the brain into the cerebral arterial circle. From the cerebral arterial circle, it spirals up and outward of the brain (Crown Chakra), then pulls in/downward from heavens (space, state of bliss). The heavenly touch of bliss focuses on the membrane's change through grey matter and some white matter, down the spine into the T1-T9 portion of the thoracic section, spreading back into the heart, back down the spine and cauldron. In that process, it spreads into the gut—in particular, the navel dantian—from the navel dantian, expanding out into the heart again. Once this happens, BOOM, BOOM, BOOM, BOOM! Fireworks happen! This can be felt in the afterlife. Not many will grasp this.

On a side note, it's very important to attend to your navel dantian daily by qigong, eating healthy, exercise and concentration, so your life force energy is not limited due to not purging the emotions from that area or exhausting memories that bring harm to our life's stability and power. It will take attention, awareness, and strictness to accomplish the clearing of your navel chakra. When the white liquid substance drips down the spine to the flora in the gut, it's important to be in a great state.

Being toxic, angry, or hostile while the white liquid substance drips down from the pineal and pituitary glands can harm others, and you will be held accountable. Polish your mind, soul, vertebrae, and the T1-T9 thoracic section of the spine by express directives. Conquest of self makes you a true master. Those who understand follow their soul into enlightenment. This type of teaching will have you open to exploring who you are, diving deep down into the abyss of you on levels most people cannot comprehend. Why not be childlike as in playful, joyous, peaceful, and graceful unto you and others?

Note: Shu can help quiet the mind of the gut.
Note: In this system, the navel is a dantian.

3 IN 1

After going around the soul once, you may be ready for the merging of the octahedron, sphere, and cube as a result of the purging and transformation that has occurred. The integration of matter, energy, and spirit helps the overall wellbeing of the soul. Matter is related to the Lower Dantian, energy is the Middle Dantian, and spirit the Upper Dantian. You will begin to feel warmth, grace, and purity in your being. The octahedron is located in front of your sternum and Middle Dantian, the sphere is located at your Upper Dantian, and the cube is located at your Lower Dantian. As you practice this exercise, the merging will begin to take place. This shift will have a significant effect on your feelings, stability, power, awareness, and divine connection. You will begin to operate at a higher frequency experiencing another level of awareness. These exercises can be done every day.

Face the window where the sun is pouring in or outside and begin the following steps:

Stand up.

Inhale into the transmutation area, filling it with joy three times in a row.

From the transmutation area, send joy to the ridicule area three times in a row.

Inhale into the transmutation area, filling it with joy one time.

From the transmutation area, send joy to the sustenance area three times in a row.

Inhale into the transmutation area, filling it with joy one time.

From the transmutation area, send joy to the turmoil area three times in a row.

Move on to the next feeling.

Inhale into the transmutation area, filling it with peace three times in a row.

From the transmutation area, send peace to the ridicule area three times in a row.

Inhale into the transmutation area, filling it with peace one time.

From the transmutation area, send peace to the sustenance area three times in a row.

Inhale into the transmutation area, filling it with peace one time.

From the transmutation area, send peace to the turmoil area three times in a row.

Move on to the next feeling.

Inhale into the transmutation area, filling it with grace three times in a row.

From the transmutation area, send grace to the ridicule area three times in a row.

Inhale into the transmutation area, filling it with grace one time.

From the transmutation area, send grace to the sustenance area three times in a row.

Inhale into the transmutation area, filling it with grace one time.

From the transmutation area, send grace to the turmoil area three times in a row.

Lie with your chest on the ground.

Inhale into the transmutation area, filling it with joy three times in a row.

From the transmutation area, send joy to the ridicule area three times in a row.

Inhale into the transmutation area, filling it with joy one time.

From the transmutation area, send joy to the sustenance area three times in a row.

Inhale into the transmutation area, filling it with joy one time.

From the transmutation area, send joy to the turmoil area three times in a row.

Move on to the next feeling.

Inhale into the transmutation area, filling it with peace three times in a row.

From the transmutation area, send peace to the ridicule area three times in a row.

Inhale into the transmutation area, filling it with peace one time.

From the transmutation area, send peace to the sustenance area three times in a row.

Inhale into the transmutation area, filling it with peace one time.

From the transmutation area, send peace to the turmoil area three times in a row.

Inhale into the transmutation area, filling it with grace three times in a row.

From the transmutation area, send grace to the ridicule three times in a row.

Inhale into the transmutation area, filling it with grace one time

From the transmutation area, send grace to the sustenance area three times in a row.

Inhale into the transmutation area, filling it with grace one time

From the transmutation area, send grace to the turmoil area three times in a row.

Inhale into the transmutation area, filling it with joy three times in a row.

From the transmutation area, send joy to the ridicule area three times in a row.

Inhale into the transmutation area, filling it with joy one time.

From the transmutation area, send joy to the sustenance area three times in a row.

Inhale into the transmutation area, filling it with joy one time.

From the transmutation area, send joy to the turmoil area three times in a row.

Inhale into the transmutation area, filling it with peace three times in a row.

From the transmutation area, send peace to the ridicule area three times in a row.

Inhale into the transmutation area, filling it with peace one time.

From the transmutation area, send peace to the sustenance area three times in a row.

Inhale into the transmutation area, filling it with peace one time.

From the transmutation area, send peace to the turmoil area three times in a row.

Move on to the next feeling.

Inhale into the transmutation area, filling it with grace three times in a row.

From the transmutation area, send grace to the ridicule area three times in a row.

Inhale into the transmutation area, filling it with grace one time.

From the transmutation area, send grace to the sustenance area three times in a row.

Inhale into the transmutation area, filling it with grace one time.

From the transmutation area, send grace to the turmoil area three times in a row.

QUALITY REIGN SUPREME

LIGHT

After going around the soul once or clearing out the sections of your heart enough, and grasping the importance of joy, grace, and peace, in meditation, a small white light will appear in your heart, usually in the transmutation area. Smile into the light and ask it to expose matters of your heart that need to be worked out. The light that appears in the heart will show your inner truth. Eventually, the whole heart will become full of light so long as you are grasping the work that is taking place within and around you.

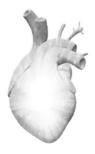

Smile pleasantly, peacefully, gracefully, and joyfully in the light of your heart holding that smile/feelings. Clinch your perineum muscles, inhaling and exhaling into the light, allowing the rays to reach out in the quantum field. Remember, this is part of your essence. The light being of yourself has emerged by accessing this part of you into the quantum field and will shatter your existence as you know it.

Inhale into the transmutation area, filling it with joy, peace, and grace.

From the transmutation area, send joy, peace, and grace to the ridicule area.

From the transmutation area, send joy, peace, and grace to the sustenance area.

From the transmutation area, send joy, peace, and grace to the turmoil area.

Inhale down to your whole heart, turning it into pure light by merging and holding the three feelings of joy, peace, and grace. From your mind, visualize what you want to manifest, have it drop down into your heart, then combine the visualization and feeling of what you want to manifest. Hold that feeling and image as the light of your heart, then send that frequency to attract that goal into your life. Speak it into existence from the sternum, ending with a strong Hhhaaaaaassshhhuuu!!! This works with prayer, healing, manifestation, etc.

Eventually, the whole heart becomes light, and everything from the bottom of the spine to the top of the head becomes light. Give it direction. The different aspects of your soul will begin to illuminate. Joy, grace, and peace are a part of the "bird heart." Hence the saying "heart light as a feather." The lighter the heart is, it will give you access to interdimensions. Your light being can intersect multidimensions and planes. The more you experience different dimensions, the more you will learn how to deal with the situation more effectively.

You need a strong heart to get to your diamond light body. The three levels of The Integration System are highly suggested to be completed before going into the diamond light body. For some, the Integration System will integrate on its own into the diamond light body if you allow that to happen. By the time you thoroughly go through all the exercises in this book with quality—which may take you one or two years— you will have a heart of gold. Remember to teach from the heart, speak from the heart, and gather from the heart. The heart is the wisest place to begin bonds and strengthen relationships. The heart is the wisest place to be. Quality reigns supreme.

QUALITY REIGN SUPREME

PROSPERITY BREATH

Center into your heart, then shift awareness to the prosperity area of the heart. Once awareness is shifted, smile while feeling prosperity in that area. Let the feeling build up, getting stronger and stronger. Inhale through the nose, down into the back of the prosperity area of the heart. Exhale the prosperity energy out of the front of the heart. Repeat over and over for at least fifteen minutes a day for thirty days straight. Once that's complete, perform at your will.

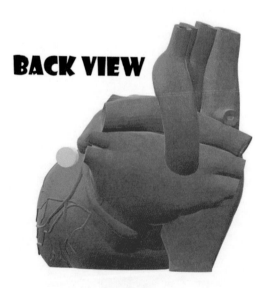

BACK VIEW

FRONT VIEW

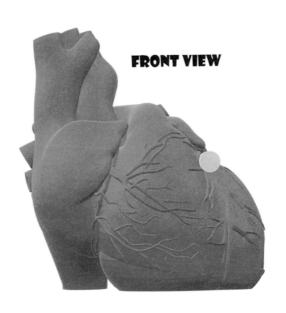

LEFT SIDE VIEW

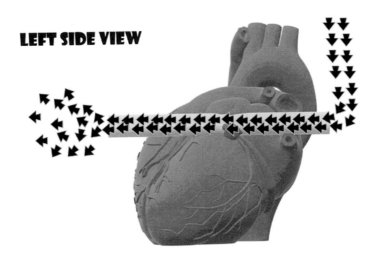

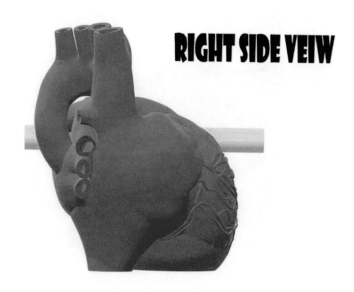

RIGHT SIDE VEIW

QUALITY REIGN SUPREME

COUPLES

This next section is for couples that have a special heartfelt connection. Please do not lie to yourself about your relationship. You know if there is an unexplainable, energetic, heartfelt connection. With that being said, both partners should be open to one another. In sharing spiritual moments with each other, I ask of you all, do not take these moments for granted. These practices will guide you two into the lessons you all need to learn and the purpose of your union with each other. You all will share many beautiful moments that will bring out the best in the two of you as well as the "shadow self" to be worked on. Remember to let go of all conditioning regarding how to relate to each other so you may have a more profound experience in intimacy. I highly encourage you to hang in there. Don't let your triggers get the best of you be

cause a new energy is experienced when the intelligence of the heart and souls come together.

Relax into your body, heart, and soul for nature to reveal more knowledge upon you two. Remember, not one partner is 100% responsible for the quality of intimacy in a relationship. Both of you must continue to stay present in the moment that will take you deeper into the many levels of intimacy. When anger, ego, and complacency set in, remember to perform these practices. Doing so will take you further than what's written in this book. Also, keep in mind that there are forces—some invisible—that do not want to see you grow for the better, especially as a couple. The forces that I speak of are unconsciousness, unhappiness, confusion, and spirits that feed off of many energetic vibrations that can keep you away from your true nature. These practices will help alleviate these forces, but it may not be easy all the time.

Soul integration will allow you access to just about all creation, such as the many aspects of you, i.e., energy bodies, plains, realms, nature, and others, to name a few. While learning what it's like to become whole and operate from that state of being, you will begin to understand why certain souls should not intertwine with each other for various reasons; i.e., they are vibrating on different levels that may not be conducive to one another; one soul may be detached, and the other may be whole; one soul may have many entities inside of it, causing so much confusion each lifetime, while the other doesn't and has more clarity in life. These are a few examples. Remember, quality reign supreme.

Raise the vibration in self, which will raise the vibration of the relationship. Remember to be present doing the work. Try not to run from your fears. Speak to each other from the heart and soul. Love from the heart and soul. Learn from the experience of coming together, making love from the soul. While sharing the energy and gifts from each other's souls, you two will naturally begin to prepare each other for godhood and the god state. Intimacy like this is rarely seen and taught. These teachings are going to help your soul explode into illumination, which is very powerful, intense, and emotional. Hang in there when it gets dramatic (emotionally). Create space and healthy love for self and one another.

Note: Do not place yourself in physical harm for anyone.

HEART TO HEART COMMUNICATION

1 a. Face each other while placing your awareness in your hearts. Relax and breathe in through your nose and out your mouth. Continue to breathe until your mind is quiet. Feel your heartbeat loud and clear. Once you feel your heartbeat loud and clear, focus on the pulse of the heart, giving and receiving communication from each other's heart. Let your bodies move however they are guided while the hearts communicate with another. Just continue to be present in that moment and feel what's being expressed. After both of you get the hang of this exercise, move on to the next step.

1b. As the hearts communicate with each other from the previous steps, from your sternums, energetically project out a huge octahedron. It should be big enough that you can see yourselves sitting inside one huge octahedron that you have merged together. Feel the energy of the octahedron around you while your hearts are connected without the interference of your egos. Begin to have a heart to heart convocation, fully expressing yourselves. Once you have mastered this form of intimacy, get creative with this space. For example, hold this space together in the heart while you both have orgasms to manifest whatever goals you two have, but be sure to focus on one goal at a time.

Note: This is a great space to work out communication issues with one another.

SOUL CONNECTION

Sit in front of each other while placing your awareness inside of your dantians. Let your bodies move however they feel. Begin to let the energy project out into one another, surrendering to each other. This can be intense or very subtle. Let the communication from the soul guide you two into movement and dance. Relax and go with the flow.

Examples of going with the flow—see below.

Once this connection is made, you both may be guided to start connecting the various points on the body with each other by physically touching the dantians. Both of you will experience something very powerful with each other. The dantians are also pathways to travel into different states. I won't tell you too much. I will let you two find out as you consistently do the work.

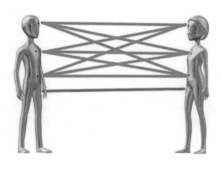

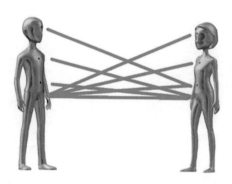

End of Level 1 of 3 Integration System

REFERENCES

https://journals.plos.org/plosone/article?id=10.1371/journ
al.pone.0150757

https://www.washingtonpost.com/news/inspired-
life/wp/2015/05/26/harvard-neuroscientist-meditation-
not-only-reduces-stress-it-literally-changes-your-
brain/?noredirect=on&utm_term=.4a2cd825e2fd

The Tantric way to personal magnetism and the projection
of charisma by sunyata saraswati

Metu neter vol 1 The great oracle of Tehuti and the
Egyptian system of spiritual civilization, Author Ra un nefer
amen, publisher khamit Corporation 1990

God man the word made flesh by Dr George W. Carey and
Inez Eudora Perry Published by the chemistry of life Co. Los
Angles California 1920

Webmd.com for serotonin

https://www.psychologytoday.com/us/blog/evolutionary-
psychiatry/201105/sunlight-sugar-and-serotonin

The nine eyes of light, ascension keys from Egypt, padma
aon prakasha, North Atlantic Books Berkeley California

Made in the USA
Columbia, SC
16 April 2022

59078862R00060